THE OLD CHORE

poems by

John Hildebidle

Typeset by Jeffrey Schwartz
Paste-up by Ed Hogan/Aspect Composition

I owe thanks especially to Margo Lockwood, for years of
encouragement; to James Richardson, Susan Goodspeed, and
the Bow and Arrow Press, for various sorts of help; to my son
Nicholas John for keeping reality more fully in my view; and
to the editors of the following publications, in which some of
these poems first appeared:
*Aspect, Beloit Poetry Journal, Green House, Harvard Magazine,
The Little Magazine, Ploughshares, Poetry Miscellany, Poetry
Northwest,* and *Southern Poetry Review.*

The publication of this book was made possible with support from the
Massachusetts Council on the Arts and Humanities, a state agency whose
funds are recommended by the Governor and appropriated by the State
Legislature.

Library of Congress Catalogue Card Number 80-70828
ISBN 0-914086-34-0
Printed in the United States of America.

Alice James Books are published by Alice James Poetry
Cooperative, Inc.

Alice James Books
138 Mount Auburn Street
Cambridge, Massachusetts 02138

for Niki
and for my mother and father

CONTENTS

marking in open air

in a country of right angles

in praise of corners

marking in open air

BONE MENDER

The bone mender
my doctor father let tend roses
in some waste land behind his office
limped around in grim clothes
old as the rocks, smelling of sheep dip,
his fingers twisted like the roots
of his prize bush; and he said
nothing, nothing at all,
but when the damp sank in your bones
for a half of mild he'd walk
up and down your back, and cure you.
They came even from Cork city to see him,
he had the healing; and once
when I was seven and screamed so
while my father tried to set a finger
I'd broken falling off a stile
he said *All right then,*
the hell with you, and next time
you can go to the bone mender
who was just then outside the window
pruning, bent over the plants
that flared bright pink
against all the green and stone,
with his back to the wind
that had blown in a hurry
all the way from Dingle
and from the look of it
didn't care either way.

MONET AT GIVERNY

Grown to secure and vivid middle age,
old enough at last to ignore the city,
his eyes even then and forty years later
shadowed in the hollows of his face
like secret weapons,

he moved to this high narrow house and laid out
such indulgent gardens to build paintings on—
never a garden with so little green—
and went each morning to the river junction
where the backlight was precisely as he wanted
to paint again and again the thumb of misted sky
between river willows—

what he saw was ever a sequence of lights,
running from one canvas to the next
to catch how the haystacks moved with light and season
from the red of poppies to hard grey,
not alive but utterly a part of things;
or to watch the poplars that, good bourgeois,
he bought where they stood so he could paint them
in an air of blue and coral,

marking in open air small changes
untouched by the accumulating large ones,
a dead son, age, the cataracts, the tumor:
he kept his eye to the last, painting
endless water lilies with an angle of sight
accurate beyond edge or shape or detail.

LOWELL READING

Everyone seems to know him,
to expect a nod of recognition
on his way up to the podium,
stooped, oddly diffident;
that heavy rusted thing reputation
hangs on him like an old suit
too well-worn to throw out.

He reads "Lepke" and a poem to Berryman
and "My Last Afternoon with Uncle Devereux"
and stops to identify each cousin.
The crowd acts as if it's no news to them.
Even when the words on the page
hold no possible laughter, he laughs,
interrupting in mid-sentence to explain the joke
in a voice almost Southern, softened
perhaps by Ireland, perhaps by living or practice,
a voice so unlikely to surprise.

The dark varnished wood of the stage
has in the dim light the glow
of old museum cases, as he looms there
like a naturalist not quite used to lecturing,
this tall, bent, aging, gentle man
who holds his battered mind at arm's length
to puzzle its peculiar anguish into speech,
and smiles as if there is something
absolute and calming he would tell us all
if we didn't know so much, if
the accident of words could bear the weight.

L'ENFANT SAUVAGE, AFTER

Since old Itard left there is no one here
who can properly say the noise
that is the wild one's name.
In the old days they came in crowds,
grey-faced men in black frock coats,
to measure the scars, to ask who his father was,
and why he smelled new snow.
By the time he understood the questions
he had no answers, and they'd made their own.

Itard and he spent the long years' work
civilizing him. He learned to beg milk,
to wear shoes and a white shirt,
not to eat with fingers or run on all fours,
how to fetch keys and set the table.
In time he no longer laughed in hard rain.

Itard wondered if he missed the old way.
He was alone then, and cold (although
he didn't know it; Itard taught him hot and cold).
Now he is still alone, but at least living.
He must know if he'd stayed wild
today he would be scandalous and dead.

The worst time was not then or now,
but the months in the dark school with the children
who grunted and wrote in the air with their hands
and poked to see if he would tear,
and never smiled, except beginning to laugh.

He is too old to bear grudges,
or to drink from the mirror of his own face
in a stream. He is used to tea now
and high-collared suits, and blankets.
The house and he get on well.
There is a park not far away
where he walks in fine weather without shoes;
and every day he thinks of the old Master
who made him this thing he was not,
then left him to live his own way through it.

NEXT DOOR

Along this river road of well-kept lawns
his loose-shingled house stands out,
less an occupation, just north of shabby—
window frames painted three shades of tan,
garage sagging, half the shutters down.
The neighbors mutter about calling in the law
to protect their equity, but never quite
get to it. Instead they wish, privately,
he'd die. It is something the old man
does not appear to think about.

He sits for hours in a wicker chair
on a porch that seems uncertain whether
it can still bear its own weight,
talking to his five dogs (all strays)
and to a skein of crows on the roofline
who grow fat as if by sucking air.
When he tells them about telephones and busses
in a language devised for shepherds,
the neighbors hear him and say
it's the old country causes the whole mess.

But he talks to none of us, not even me;
lives on as a stubborn discourtesy,
in expectation neither of outrage nor elation,
full of no virtues except pure lasting,
without contact or end, without the family
the neighbors say he had once,
which hasn't visited since I've been here,
as if they too found him annoying

or perhaps left him behind to season
like the oak logs put down for centuries
in the swamp mud of French rivers
by a tribe convinced that someone with a familiar name
would stop by every millennium or so
wanting the frame timbers of an abbey church.

SOME WOMEN IN HIS LIFE

Calypso

I might have known you'd stay husband.
You had its signs on you from the start,
like the pips of an old chicken pox—
an absolute preference for one side of the bed
you must have learned from long compromise.

Oh, it was pleasant enough, no mistake,
tricking you into using words full of p's
so you always mumbled with a guilty look,
or counting the times you told the same story
about the sea-view from your window
and never mentioned who'd snored beside you.
Don't assume I'm surprised now, or believe
all this talk about a mission or your son—
it's her, as it always has been
because you haven't the energy, old man,
to give your life a new shape and name.

So go back with my blessing
to dull considerate suet-thighed Penelope;
that old coat will never itch you awake.
The skin beneath her fallen breasts will be
wrinkled as an old chart, and her voice
so used to saying polite inconsequential things
will crack like a twig trying to mouth your name.

I wish I could see it.
Even in the dark she won't feel the same.
Healthy as you are you'll have a long long time
to feel your mind cramp from trying to tell yourself
you don't regret the long sail back to the ordinary.

Penelope

A year is the time it takes one spring
to forget the last. Ten of those
you spent off fighting for your honor
and someone else's whore. The boy grew up
so like you it was almost more than I could do
to keep him from my bed. Ten years

I watched the skin of my cheeks each day
grow a little drier. I had nothing to do but age
and watch myself age and see the boy
come closer to the day when he could leave
some woman of his own. I moved the bed into a corner
and kept my back against the cold wall
to cure the shape and pressure of your hand.

I said *Each day I will recall one of his faults,
and make it, if I can, a sin, a disease*
but it was another way of keeping you in mind
down to the scratch of your coarse thumbnail
when your hand strolled like an old watchman
up the inside of my thigh. Ten years

and then the others came home, dirty and tired
and so proud of themselves for all the blood and time.
They were kind, in their way. They said *He'll be here
in his own time.* It was worse when I believed them.
The suitors, the silly boys you butchered in the courtyard,
arrived in troops and thought they were so clever.
You needn't have worried. They wore more perfume
than I did, and damn you, even the fifteen-years-stale
recollection of you made me smile more in the nights
than anything their bodies could offer.

And now you're back, and what have we to say?
I can see the scars of other women's hands on you.
That's no surprise; you like to tell yourself
you have your needs, like eating. I'll make you
work your way back, be sure of it—be king and father
in the time I need to rest. I will make you back
into that hard young king who sailed off in gaudy armor
promising a quick war and a long peace.
If I let you sleep at all it will only be to wake you again
in the moonlight, and see on your face the love
that was there when you came through the door just now
and twenty years' waiting twisted my insides
until I could only kiss you or yelp with pain.
I loved and love you more than we both deserve.

KARL WALLENDA, MARCH, 1978

I.

At such an age will is more sure than hands,
hands more sure than balance,
neither more certain
than the truth of a long fall.
It was no failure of the old skill;
he sat quite gracefully down on the swaying wire
but the wind would not so easily
be satisfied.
He did not drop the pole
his hands knew he would need again.
When he lost his grip on the wire
he bore the heavy tool
down those hundred feet or so
that to him had stood only as measurement,
no more than the inches below
the training wire he
conquered before he could read.
Falling, he lost his element.

II.

Always before there were two facts only,
the wire and the air above it which today
tricking itself out as wind the old enemy
took on shape and time to scramble
the trained precise repeated movement,
although his falling body was still as if on the wire
poised without gesture in baggy salesman's
trousers and white shirt, and even after
the hard shock of the pavement he lay easily
like an old man struck down in traffic
he was no longer spry enough to dodge,
hurt more than anything by surprise.

III.

Once he had seen a fall in his children's faces:
that pyramid which was the sign and lifework
of the family shook once, so slightly,
then broke from geometry into bodies;
and yet he did again what he had done,
since it was just one fact that might or might not
occur again and was anyway an unthought part
of each step he had ever taken in a life
that had no past, no future, only this now,
this next step; his as surely as his hands were,
his and his father's and before him
in a place where all that mattered
was knowing his own body so completely
down to the barest vein and nail
that it was an abstraction balanced
on these soft black slippers on this wire.

FOR MY NEIGHBOR DELGADO

In this heat
the wind is nothing but a tease.
The window curtains bow out,
cajole you to lean on the sill
as if there were air.

The young girls in halters
walk slowly up the block.
The crab man at the corner
has sold his stock
but has no energy just now
to pull his wagon home
and sits on the curb with half a beer.
It will be dark soon,
but no cooler;
and you will sit up watching
half the night,
each breath hard to find.

In the old days, the old country,
before your eyes lost that white
of clay houses when the sun fades,
your hands could weave nets even in dusk light.
Loud over the hiss of waves
came the voices of the women cooking.
The cool stone streets climbed from the seawall
where boats lay upturned like sleeping creatures;
and always the wind, the smell of salt and old wood,
the moon an ice image of the sun
rising from the dark arbors on the mountain;
and at last the bright cold morning.

THE MASTERY OF THE KNUCKLEBALL

for Hoyt Wilhelm and W. C. Williams

To govern so
the concrete in motion
with the most tenuous of grips

to force as much by will as act
the erratic
to hold within determined
form

to summon
with an easy minimalist grace
the capacity repeatedly
to baffle:

it is the refuge
of the fortunately old,
who bear on even past its time
the childish craving to perform
and add the calm of long practice,
the energy of age,
a faint amusement,
and the certainty
that at some expected
but surprising moment
the gift (like all,
like breath) will fail.

AUNT FAITH

Even bruises do for sauce, she says,
hunting windfall the dogs haven't eaten
under the apple that bears one summer in three,
fruiting so heavy the thick grass

has to be walked slowly, with an eye out
for the hard early Gravensteins
shaken by boys who play trapeze.
This once, knowing apples as she does,

knowing this tree from the time she
helped set it out, she takes her share
of the work again as full partner, favoring
ones on the boarded wellhead, patient

to make fine choices, which for the sauce bag,
which for pies. She is of an age
bearing two bodies, hips and legs thickened
where the flesh has slipped down

from too-long standing, the thin girl's shoulders
curved as if she were shy about what force she has left
for talking to and about apples in a loud voice
deafness has taken all embarrassment out of—

*You lift that sack and follow this old lady once
and you'll have good eating from it, I swear,*
while she stops a little to rest
and take advantage of a good sun.

in a country of right angles

THE CITY IS A SHRUB OF WONDERS

Mistress Anne Pollard recalls her arrival in Boston

We ate the wild blueberries
that grow like dark underfur
in the tall grass on the slope of Fort Hill.
The water had the bright taste
of moss and old stone, so sweet
after the brackish mudwells of Salem.

Hermit Blaxton regretted
he'd invited us; he liked
preaching to his bull, and much
preferred marsh grass to people.
He removed down to the Narragansett,
bewailing his bad judgment—
They dump their slops in the street.
You wouldn't know the place,
all those blank salt-grey houses,
the harbor growing masts like dead spiked ferns.

Houses and masts came later.
We lived beneath Trimountain
in tents and hide wikiups,
dragging wood from the mainland.
My sister died of scurvy
while the town cove was sealed with pale blue ice.
We doted on small blessings,
no wolves, no rattlesnakes, no
mosquitoes. The spring came late,
after thick rains. Off mudflats
the river coiled new weeds,
smelling of salt, and fish, and rosemary.

THE SUPPLICATION OF DOROTHY BRADFORD

> *Being thus arrived in a good harbor*
> *and brought safe to land,*
> *they fell upon their knees.*
> Of Plimouth Plantation

Being thus far borne
and no further,
into this cold dead place;
and if those low white dunes
that rise up like a very beast
or the great sea-eagle
crying to the snow
be God's mercy? No,
only beasts here for us,
wallowed together all those weeks,
all men beasts here,
scrambling on our knees
for food—where in this
is providence? We are all
fools, all children;
yet to be children,
still to have the hope
that drove us
from the sometime home of Leyden,
to wander on this sand
God-given to His chosen
as a test, and such of grace
as brings only a salt spray
frozen as glass on our hair—
no haven here for we unworthy,
some of us, me alone perhaps;

but not so, I see it
in faces: death, a prophecy,
even now it walks here,
I see it in the faces
and the grey oak that bore us
bitten by the salt air
as we chose in all our pride
to be Chosen, and to die
in choosing: death
even as a light
in the wilderness I see it,
not grace but punishment,
here now it stands before us
and we will surely die.

The wind is cold,
cold, it bites to the heart;
and the sea white with shoal
as the eye of God turning away:
no haven, no succor
from wind and the salt sand
that gives no root—
thus far the choice has carried us
and will bear no further:

> *O Christ Jesus,*
> *will you come to me;*
> *if I cry in a voice*
> *fierce as the gull's,*
> *if I cry to you*
> *will you come to me*
> *as I walk out*
> *on this cold grey water?*

SHAKER BOX

The wonder is that anyone
would live in such detail
until the order of a mitred
joint bore the soul's burden
to a light circle of talking

spirits singing with Mother Ann
in drawings of the Tree,
the Fruit, and promised, to a God
who delighted to be
danced to, the lifted gifts of hands

packed each one inside the next like
the nests of creation,
held sure and absolute by grace,
the maker's eye, and no-
thing so approximate as nails.

GREAT AMERICAN DESERT

To stake it all on this one chance,
this indecisive river trail, was his idea.
I don't complain, at least not to him.
There is too much time here for regret.
Once planted it chokes the land.

Yesterday we travelled sixteen hours
and saw no tree worth the name.
This place has no defining edge,
only space too large for any use.
It is pointless to long for the mediation
of a ridge or a stand of timber
or the stone wall that marked the far edge
of cleared land behind the house.
If you live long enough, they say,
the mountains rise up like a fever.

He walks well ahead. Scouting, he says.
He tastes less of the dust
and can see for miles and miles
and still see only what he carries in his head.
A promise, he says. A new Kentucky,
clear, unpeopled, and all waiting, a double
of the place he did not love well enough to keep.
He walks well ahead with his dream.
The rest of us are sucked forward
like dropped paper in a ship's wake.

The old time is gone. Since west and east
are no different, the sun has no direction.
Noon here goes on almost to nightfall.
Now barely past spring we think only of winter,
the winter in the mountains. No other time matters.

He said, we'll go; and I nodded.
I had no reasons to stand his.
Now I won't forgive that nod.

Interminable twin tracks and scars of dead fires
mark the trail; and of course the dead—
my sister dead of camp cholera, and the young one
bitten by a snake, and the others whose names
I never learned, dead of dust and bad water
and too much looking back. The old die first,
and the very young, and the ones
with a clumsy hopeless spirit,
or the ones without luck, men no less than women;
fast, slow, it's the same death,
all one burial, with no stones for markers.
What with the wind and scavengers and rain and grass
the graves go back to prairie in a day or so;
but of the dying there are always enough
to keep the road clear.

I don't talk to him about death.
He does not think it helps to think about it.
He has dreams, and does not care to know
it is dreams that kill, and their dreamers,
and they never die alone.

THE DEACON'S PLACE

Because the steep ridge slope gave no footing
he built closer to the river bottom
than he wanted. The land he'd bought blind;
and they got there so late in the season,
he put the house up fast and small. One room,
a barn the same size, a dog trot; timbers
he dragged himself from a stand of red oak
half a mile away. When the autumn fogs
boiled out of canebrakes the house was so squat
and so dark with pine pitch it disappeared.
Its angles stood a little out of true,
but it was sound enough, drier than tents.

The cleared land spread grudgingly uphill.
Soil jerked awake with the new prod of seeds.
The house thrust out ells like a runner vine,
and each one bore the same signs of his work,
as recognizable as his children;
but he set no special meaning in that,
there was no call for gloating about facts.
The big flood pushed a dark mud discolor
halfway and further up the chimney piece.
He rode it out and rebuilt what had dropped,
just as before, but now with his sons' help.

Those same sons called the house too small, too grim.
He never complained or moved, and in time
when winter stripped the woods he could see
his children's white two-storied houses
downstream, at the river bend near town.
He asked to be buried beneath the floor
he whitewashed every spring for all those years
long after the wife he did it for died.
Instead the children put him in the plot
he'd cut out for her from the ridgetop scrub.

Empty, the house sagged on in its old way.
Children—great-grandchildren now, or strangers—
went there to spark, to retell ghost stories,
or when they'd gotten into dutch at home,
until a freak snow crushed the roof. Neighbors
stripped off whatever boards weren't too warped.
Before long all there was to mark the place
was the faint earthsag of the cellar hole,
a thatch of first growth that reclaimed its own
from the humus of desperate carpentry.

CZOLGOSZ THE ASSASSIN

The crazy girl-faced Slavic boy
who loved Red Emma Goldman
though she didn't know his name,
waited with the rest in the reception line
with a pistol in his bandaged hand.

He had his reasons.
The anarchists said he was a spy
sent to stir up trouble,
though they thought the act was useful.
The Hearst papers wanted him
staked out for the ants.
Red Emma tried to remember if she'd met him,
tried to send a message, offered
to nurse the President (he hung on
for a week). They wouldn't let her near
either one of them.

Czolgosz waited and showed no
impatience, and when the time came
he was so close he couldn't miss.
At his trial the marks of prison beatings showed,
but all he said was
I did it for the people. When he fried,
the papers cheered, typesetters
cursed him, Red Emma cried a bit
and dreamed of his pale imprisoned face,
his crazy eyes; and there was no one
who knew him well, or even how to say his name.

DAY WORK

First the number four trolley crosstown
past the stores with their windows
frosted hard, past the courthouse and the park,
the bronze soldier hip-deep in snow,
to the wide streets of belly-front houses—

an hour's trip, and another half hour until
her hands warmed enough to work the needle
to cure the rip in the drapes as smooth
as butter on a new burn, a skill
they could find a month's work for, more or less.

They liked that she was clean and not flirty.
They liked, now the sun left so early,
that she worked as well by lamplight as daylight
and never mind the headaches. They liked that she
kept her eyes off the silver and the aquavit

and ate without a fuss cold soup or cheese or
day-old bread which they really didn't have to give her,
it wasn't part of the bargain. Going home nights
the motorman, proud of his buttons and the fur
cap he pulled off to greet her, made eyes,

full of talk about the Dakota farm he was after
(and bought, in ten years; and went bust in five more,
a good proud noisy tall impractical smiling fellow
with forearms like breadloaves she remembered from summer
when he rolled his sleeves back to show them off;

who lost money like a pine tree sheds cones).
They were both waiting for him to raise the gumption
to talk seriously about a life together (spent past the time
his teeth and his good humor and then
finally his eyes went so she had to lead him

around by the hand and he stopped laughing about years ago
when she was such a pretty squint-eyed thing—she knew
she was never pretty, but let him talk, let it mark out
this life from another, either to be worn like a borrowed
shirtwaist at a certain distance from the body

or it might snag and tear and need paying for)—
but for now only the old long ride, sore-
eyed, past the winter's usual frozen details,
past the park where the snowed-in soldier
still numbered his inconspicuous dead.

BIOGRAPHY

What record the great world has of her
is the night he glanced in a crowded loge
at the dress she borrowed for the occasion
the color he thought of silk radishes
and hoarded it for a rich line or two.

He who did no more than write of strangers
wasn't introduced although temptation
hung a long while in his eye, and she
not knowing she had from a distance
suffered an accident of contact
went home smiling in spite of a headache

on the arm of a boy she'd already
decided was marriageable, who'd love her
beyond what he then suspected was
his capacity, and grown in time
prosperous, would have her sit for a portrait
that came no closer than words to holding
the texture of skin her children loved
even when it had gone slack with age.

When near the end the scholar discovered her
propped in a beach chair watching the catboats
belly in the shoals near the causeway
she still had in the sunlight the same smile.
The dress she remembered, and the headache,
the play vaguely, the intermission not at all.

RELICS

John L. Sullivan, in old age, in his arbor

The Boston Strong Boy chomps a dead stogey.
Hamfisted, barrelbellied monument,
in his grey and honored age he is serene
and tends his leafy plants this bright autumn.
His broad open Irish face bears no mark,
not from Paddy Ryan, not from Corbett,
not from Bare-Knuckle Kilrain or the rest—
in his time he could take the hardest punch.
He always did his job of work, laying brick
or slugging for the title or even
play-acting Atlas in the vaudeville—
the great John L. gave you your nickel's worth,
a fine example to his noisy race.
So bighearted, honest, plainspoken, tough
but as his vines show, sensitive, he asked
no favors but took no cheap advantage,
kept his nose clean and bought his share of rounds,
and now, reformed, preaches for Temperance.
He scrapped his way into the history books
by beating proud men bloody with his fists.

Herbert Hoover flyfishing for trout,
Klamath River, California, 1933

Anger shortens the breath and lets the body
go its own way, unwilled. You cannot fish
in anger. He does not. His stiff smile is ready

to acknowledge that the world refused the touch
of his controlling hand. Fish line is easier.
Fishing follows rules. That so much

time could be thought well-spent whether
or not the steelhead strike, is a rule.
Waiting is a rule. Fishing, for a clever

man certain of his own footing, is full
of the rich pleasures of cause-and-effect,
stretched calmly over the indefinite pool

of spring water and long afternoons. Let
the line rest in easy irregular loops
on the surface. Let the rod, a perfect

thin curve in the air, be sharp visible proof
of the steadiness of your hand and mind.
Let the world know you can wait, aloof

and cheery and confident and full of benign
foreknowledge of the nature of things.
Wait and the fish will strike, the line

will bear the weight of tonight's supper, in time;
or tomorrow's or some day's. Wait, he always
said; my dear children, wait. It will be fine.

Just be patient a little longer, and one of these days
it will all work out. Wait. Soon. One day.

FOR HARRIET QUIMBY, AVIATRIX: JULY 1, 1912

Harriet, she of the dark eyes and prim name,
strolled in her black leather across the tamped wastelot
to the contraption the farmboys gawked at
which she liked to call an aeroplane

and chatted briefly about the weather
which had shown no sign at all of breaking,
the thick morning air heavy enough to walk on
and even a breeze blown in specially from the Azores

not the slightest relief to the men, bank-clerks
judging by their stiff suits, who made jokes
about skirts in a high wind, while Harriet
tied her scarf like a bunting around her neck

and managed a quick but arresting smile
for the guy taking pictures for the *Advertiser*
before strapping herself in and pointing in her usual
direct way straight toward the harbor,

rising eventually into real, unexpected air,
high enough that the gentlemen's cigars went out
unnoticed in their hands; and then while the crowd
was still wondering what it must look like from up there

she twitched in mid-loop like a shot hawk, went wing-over,
fell, irreconcilably upside down, and hit,
tumbling like a crumpled map toward the breakwater,
all with a great noise, of lament and snapping wood.

THE CHILD IN THE HOUSE

The day Lindbergh took off for le Bourget
in Baltimore it rained just after noon
but didn't break the heat. The water
burned off pavement in a cloud,
and all the brick row houses heated up like kilns.
Not summer yet, but nearly.

They got home late from work.
The child, left all day with neighbors,
was sick and went to bed. They sat over supper
not facing each other across the kitchen table.
He said (the third time) he'd move out.
She said that was his business
so long as he sent money every month.
Back and forth they threw the blame
for the child the forceps ruined, dead a year.
She said both kids were mistakes
then went up to take a bath.
He went through the paper, back to front,
and saved the front page when he finished.

Upstairs, the child, not five, still
not asleep, curled around her sore stomach
and the ceramic angel left from Christmas,
and listened to the voices in the street.
She wondered just who Lucky Lindy was
and if perhaps he'd ever come to visit.

POTATO LANDSCAPE

In the long grey hours
between crops
these are the names
to be given
a potato's dying:

Leaf Roll. Mosaic.
Late Blight. Yellow Dwarf.
Black Scurf. Sunscald.
Flea Beetle. Blackleg.
Hopperburn. Wart.
Purple Top. Scab.

The cut of land turns a body.
Hills would give neck twist from looking over.
Here it is all down and draws
even the children shorter.
The ground plane breaks clean at the horizon.
The houses, crate-slat, sign-metal, tarpaper
stand sagwaisted in the rumpled fields.
What grows here by nature
is rock and catarrh and scrub
that needs pulling but is no good timber.
You start the children on that early,
and on picking rock from the dirt
when the frost clears but the loam is cold enough
to bite your fingers numb in an hour.
Your breath hangs in your face like the lint of old wool.
Your eyes look at a grey distance with no use for borders.

And these are the gaudy names
made for a small dirt-skinned fruit
in a country of right angles:

>   *Early Ohio. Pearl. Irish Cobbler.*
>   *White Rose. Pawnee. Katahdin.*
>   *Erlaine. Green Mountain. Mesaba.*
>   *Peachblow. Abundance. Triumph.*

in praise of corners

IOWA BLIZZARD: 1950

Caught driving from Burlington to Red Oak

Even as
the grey nap of the felt seat
parts to show the weave
of the fabric
or the thick frost
on the windows
grows and recedes
under my breath
or the sketch of my finger
even as the voices
of my parents in the front seat
rumble
across the hiss of the flakes
only raised
to warn me from looking
(Sit down. I told you to sit down.)
even as the voices
and the brittle scrape
of the wind
and the worn grey nap of the seat
and the silver mist on the windows
enclose (not death,
not sleep, containment)
so thick even the reach of a hand
through an opened window
could not touch
the hard sealed core—just
so the squall of white chenille
against a grey-purple rug
of sky: the storm

In the farmhouse where we stopped

In the morning:
the sun off new snow
melts the ceiling—
so bright it hurts to look out
from under a pile
of down comforters,
only my nose awake to the cold,
a sharp ice-point
swelling out of warm me,
too warm to risk
reaching out a hand
to thaw my nose,
squinting against the shriek of light
through the window:
so warm

        but if
in the way of children
calamity proceeds
so fast to luxury,
from the dark cold Buick
to this comforted bed
and the smell of breakfast,
could it not reverse,
each moment to be seen again
more starkly?

An accident on a just-plowed road

the force
of the car rolling down the slope
erases the traction of the tires
and the slow long spin begins,
the car seized by an inevitable mathematic,
my mother half-turned
to hold me in the seat,
the sun through the windows
whirling
back to front
and back again,
slowly,
as the Buick eases
toward the narrow bridge
but slides just short
into the banked shoulder
levelled by the snow—
and in the sharp thud
of the car coming to rest
the snap of my mother's wrist
against the dashboard.

Waiting for my mother and the car to heal

My father takes me to a movie—
"Sabu the Elephant Boy"

coming back, the snow piled—
how high? on either side,
a path just wide enough
for two of us to pass
like marbles down a channel,
the snow piled
almost to the second story,
the path dark from the shadows
despite the bright afternoon sun,
the snow so high
it threatens to close in
over the top, to fall
of its own weight—
and terrified I am happy
with the clutch of my father's hand
to hold off collapse.

CRAZY HORSE'S ARM

All the times you went away
to cities with strange names
and came home
with a satchelful of gifts—
you told me once
how you met your father
in a diner years after
he left home for good
and talked to him
as you talk to everyone,
people in elevators,
people on planes, in stores,
in lines waiting for tickets
to a movie, a ball game:
the salesman's gift.
All your father could say
was *How've you been?*
I understood him more than you.

Or the day
you took my mother
to meet your people—
all the way to Philadelphia,
your timid fiancée, the first time
she'd ever been on a train;
and when you got to the door
you told her you'd explained to them
she was a stripper at the Gaiety
but a good girl—

or so you said.
You always told such stories:
at dinner once
in the stuccoed dining room
of the house we left that spring
you told us you'd fought at Little Big Horn,
survived, swore vengeance,
tracked down Crazy Horse himself,
and laid him low—
his arm was in the icebox
(as you always called it)
carefully preserved—Crazy Horse's Arm
all wrapped up like a roast.
I didn't buy a word of it,
until I saw the look on Johnny Good's face,
the way his eyes stared
through the kitchen door
at the white refrigerator—
and then, just for a minute, I believed.

PREMATURE ELEGY

Maybe dead you would make sense to me
in the way death has of making lives seem whole.
As a child I sometimes dreamed you dead,
just to inherit old pipes and big clothes.
I made up long and tearful deathbed speeches
to heal my annoying conscience.

Now I can't convince myself to wish you'd die,
but with you dead I'd write all the lines,
double as son and father. I'd have you
tell me why you taught me not to speak,
and I'd admit why I learned so quickly;
and we would both be free, at last,
of the old chore of loving face to face.

Then, as more and more your habits set hard in me—
bitten nails, a limp, a way with bad jokes
and other people's children—everyone who knew you
will remark how I age just as you did
and with enough time and patience
I can become the stone that marks you.

FOR A CITY WEDDING

The streets contrive an accidental show,
hawkers and jackhammers yakking
against the concrete where nothing should grow

except the potted limp geraniums set out
by the humorless city fathers as a sign of spring—
still the tough grass cracks the sidewalk grout,

finds the scar left by frost heave and thrives
in gutters where there's dirt enough to sweep.
The churchyard has sod, pleasant to foot and eye,

happy to green in thanks for a gift of water
from the caretaker's sprinkler.
It knows its place, under the clipping rigor

of his eye—the stuff of shrines and garden
cemeteries, blank as poster paint, hardly
a plant at all: a public convenience,

but it won't bear weather. So I would wish you
a weedy union, tough without water
if the season turns that way, yellow

at edges but unconcerned by it,
short on manners but long in the root,
a hardy, sharp, insistent

growing thing that prospers even in this
barely green and stony place where we live.

NOTE-OF-HAND

While I can make you what I want,
the bright gold child I've barely fathered,
I'll shout the most unlikely promises—
never, let's say, to wrap you in those
poisoned cushions fathers make their children,
not to hold against you what I imagine.
I worry that what I'll hand on most easily
will be all I'd rather junk.

Against the harder time when you're less abstract,
I prepare a bargain: use me, when you can,
as an excuse. I'll try to teach you
to trust at last eyes above ear,
touch above either, words only
on your own strict terms. I'll work
to be ready to look square at the fact of you,
matching hair for hair and wrinkle to wrinkle,
mirror, obligation, child:
to say over and over the hard word love
until the sting goes and the noise of it
swells like amazement to heal the air between us.

LAKE CONISTON

What I don't know is most of here—
that tiny pinwheel flower for instance,
nearly gone by from blue to white,
an aster maybe,
or just what I'd call a weed,
stuck in the damp woods
when everything has passed
to leaf-fall and toadstool.
Picking it for you,
I could call it stubborn or a relict
marking its fellows' passing,
but there's the good chance
it's only a flower that blooms this late
from no choice or sadness of its own.

There are books, guidebooks,
handbooks indexed by color and leaf
to give the names of things—
spikenard? the drawing
is too small to tell,
and the color wrong, white from the start;
but a late survivor
and the name would do so nicely.

Finding one thing is the missing of others.
The drizzle ruins even the field-guide's ink
and paging through
leaves no time to notice
the ground underfoot spring like an old porch step;
or to look in the sluice pool
near the mill's tumbled cellar hole,
water coal black but so clear
the white line of fallen birch
points down and down
to a bottom I have to imagine,
and more, cold and hard, to wet rock.

TO SPEAK OF THE FEAR THAT IS AUTUMN

Suddenly the dominant is brown
and all the creepers that shrill red
up the trunks of old lindens
are in key and leading.
The few greens left
have not changed in the least
but look sad now, like the last room
of a house you're moving out of,
where each dent in the wall,
to an eye that knows its business,
is notation clear as tree rings.

All logic says there'll be another spring
and we'll be here to see it,
that the last roses overripened in the side yard
are no more fatal than the first,
that circles are as common
and more true than lines;
but logic is a cold friend,
now most of all, when no leaf
can scuttle down the curb without bearing
an energy of premonition,

as if someone took the trouble
to compose this autumn
to prefigure my death, or anyone's—
God, when the jangle of mortality
gets too thick in my ears,
send me a cheap lively tune
whistled if you can manage it
by a ripe highwaisted woman,
her breasts shaking under a rough sweater,
sailing the cold wind like a catboat,
with nothing on her mind
more weighty than the play of leaves.

JANUARY THAW

This sham spring floods the burying ground,
sitting in a pool at the low corner
where the skewed headstones float like stone gulls
and losing for once their roots seem to progress

through wind ripples in the puddle
toward the clutch of black trees shading grass
matted across the family tombs.
Spring now is without the bother of growth,

without April mud since the firm ground
holds its frost line only inches down,
without any bud to unsettle
branch geometries near the wrought iron fence:

a plan of later unanalysed seasons,
the sour we need to know true goods by,
to show how close this wetting is
to the bitter grey time in November

that is never a sign of progress
because we look then so desperately
forward, past the harsh twist of the wind
and the blank flat of clouds, to a cold

due back any time. In the morning
if the freeze comes quick and hard enough
the boys will skate around these markers,
cracking their slapshots off epitaphs

as if they knew best how to deal with signs;
and the stones will settle again in ground
that is white or brown or green as the season has it
but earth in any case, the stuff of flowers waiting their time.

LATE JUNE ON THE ISLAND

When the colors first come up with the sun,
dark spring green sits well on the fiddleheads.
The marsh grass pretends to be a meadow,
and the white oak in the side yard, half dead,
manages new suckers to throw shadow
on its striplings. Each green variation
is weighted with the blue of deep water.

Of course there must be an August later,
when colors sour with heat and the air is
thick enough to fold. But this morning, this
green deserves not to be much thought over,
not to have future thrown like weed killer
on unexpected growth, but to be instead
left whole in a brief kindliness of sun.

IN PRAISE OF CORNERS

Optimism is absolutely not the point.
Believe whatever you want, whether
we'll sun together in warm reflected light;
or say, like a bitter granny,
don't trust good, it spoils—
what we can believe in is lasting,
and anyway too much sun burns the eyes.

Leave reflecting to mirrors, then;
if need be, we'll take the colder way,
to let our rough edges grate, not for pain
or smoothing, but to catch and hold
like boxes jammed in a tight hall,
stuck for good; and so the trick will be
to manage, if only once or twice,
to say the bitter thing in love's voice.

HERE

Early, while it still rained,
a leak from the bent drainpipe
rapped on some hollow
like an idle thumb on a bucket,
loud enough to batter sleep

and since the light was not
high enough to shape or color,
ear was the one sense good enough
to guide the better, touch,
toward the low huff of your breathing

where my hand drifts out of habit,
relearning the arc of possibility,
a promise strict enough to bear
time and weather and even
the dull fire of the ordinary,

hard-wearing as a sensible tweed—
O my lovely stubborn comforter,
in this place whatever life I'm due
rests easily and, if the wish holds,
for as long as I know rain or noise.